LEGENDARY LADIES
OF
BROADWAY
1960s to the 1970s

FOREWORD
by Stewart Nicholls — page 2

AND ALL THAT JAZZ
Chita Rivera — page 5 — track 1

DON'T RAIN ON MY PARADE
Barbra Streisand — page 12 — track 2

EASY TO BE HARD
Lynn Kellogg — page 24 — track 4

EVERGREEN
Barbra Streisand — page 28 — track 5

FAR FROM THE HOME I LOVE
Julia Migenes — page 34 — track 6

HEY, LOOK ME OVER
Lucille Ball — page 19 — track 3

NEVER
Madeline Kahn — page 38 — track 7

NOT WHILE I'M AROUND
Angela Lansbury — page 44 — track 8

RAINING IN MY HEART
Bernadette Peters — page 48 — track 9

ROXIE
Gwen Verdon — page 52 — track 10

SOMETHING HAS HAPPENED
Mary Martin — page 57 — track 11

SOON IT'S GONNA RAIN
Rita Gardner — page 60 — track 12

Published 2005.
© International Music Publications Ltd, Griffin House,
161 Hammersmith Road, London, W6 8BS, England.

Music recorded, arranged and engraved by Artemis Music Ltd.
(www.artemismusic.com)

Legendary Ladies of Broadway: 1960s to the 1970s *by Stewart Nicholls*

Chita Rivera
And All That Jazz from *Chicago*

Chita Rivera (b. 1933) – Lively, energetic and feisty dancer, singer and actress, Chita Rivera has had a hugely successful career on Broadway and in London. After appearing in the chorus of various Broadway musicals, Miss Rivera gained the small role of Fifi in *Seventh Heaven* (1955). She followed this with the featured role of Rita in *Mr. Wonderful*, followed by Anita in the ground breaking *West Side Story* (1957), which she re-created in London (1958). The leading role of Rose in *Bye Bye Birdie* followed in 1960 and again in London in 1961. Miss Rivera then found herself in various unsuccessful musicals that did not progress from their regional openings before returning to Broadway, as Anyanka in the short lived *Bajour* (1964). The role of Nicky in the film of *Sweet Charity* followed in 1969 before a triumph as Velma in *Chicago* on Broadway in 1975. The sequel to *Bye Bye Birdie – Bring Back Birdie* (1981) was a flop as was *Merlin* (1983) and *The Rink* (1984), although Miss Rivera won a Tony Award for the latter. Miss Rivera had much success creating the title role in *Kiss of the Spiderwoman* in London (1992) followed by winning her second Tony Award for the Broadway production (1993). Miss Rivera played the leading role of Claire Zachanassinian in a new musical: *The Visit* in Chicago in 2001, but this failed to reach Broadway. A cameo role in the film of *Chicago* (2002) was followed by Lilian Le Fleur in the Broadway revival of *Nine* (2003).

Chicago (1975)
Music by John Kander / Lyrics by Fred Ebb / Book by Fred Ebb and Bob Fosse

Chicago in the roaring 20s: Roxie Hart kills her lover and although she tries to get her ineffectual husband to take the blame, she is found out and finds herself in prison where she becomes the top dog – much to the annoyance of fellow inmate Velma Kelly. Roxie employs smarmy ace lawyer Billy Flynn to get her out of prison. He takes her on and together they manipulate the press to show Roxie in a 'good light' which will hopefully help her case. All is going well until another murder takes the press's attention and Roxie is old news. She counteracts this by announcing that she is pregnant. She is the darling of the press and Billy sings that his job is pure show business 'Razzle Dazzle'! Yet again, another person comes along with a bigger and better story. The press forget all about Roxie so she forms a double act with Velma, they cash in on their crimes and make it big in Vaudeville!

Chita Rivera created the role of Velma in *Chicago*. The story of Roxie murdering her lover is re-enacted on stage as the song **And All That Jazz** is sung by Velma to comment on the action. The recording used in this book is based on the original 1975 Broadway cast album as sung by Chita Rivera (*Arista – 07822-18952-2*).

Chicago was a moderate success in its first production on Broadway in 1975 running for 898 performances. Its London production opened in 1979 for 600 performances. A Broadway revival in 1996 became a phenomenon and prompted productions all over the world and a film (2002).

Barbra Streisand
Don't Rain On My Parade from *Funny Girl* and Evergreen from *A Star Is Born*

Barbra Streisand (b 1942) – A star actress, director, producer and writer, but primarily known for her phenomenal singing voice. Miss Streisand first appeared on the Broadway musical stage as Miss Marmelstein in the musical *I Can Get It For You Wholesale*. A recording contract followed in 1963. In 1964, Miss Streisand conquered Broadway as Fanny Brice in *Funny Girl*, a role she reprised in London (1966) and on film in 1968, winning an Academy Award. Her film career continued with the leading roles in musicals *Hello, Dolly!* (1969), *On A Clear Day You Can See Forever* (1970), *Funny Lady* (1975), *A Star Is Born* (1976), *Yentl* (1983) and many non-musical films including: *What's Up, Doc?* (1972), *The Way We Were* (1973), and *The Main Event* (1979). From the late 1970s Miss Streisand also produced, directed and wrote many of her films. Miss Streisand has starred in various concerts throughout the world and continues her successful recording career, gaining countless awards for her discs.

Funny Girl (1964)
Music by Jule Styne / Lyrics by Bob Merrill / Book by Isobel Lennart

Fanny Brice wants to be a star – much to the amusement of her neighbourhood who think that although she has talent, she does not have the looks to succeed in show business. Her audition for a musical hall is not successful - mainly because she would stand out in the chorus - but her determination impresses the dance director who works with her and before long she is performing in front of the chorus! She is spotted by handsome gambler Nicky Arnstein, who bluffs his way with the management of the musical hall and secures Fanny continued work with an excellent salary. Fanny's reputation gains her a part in "Ziegfeld Follies" where she causes a sensation by having the chutzpah to appear in a wedding song pretending to look pregnant! It is clear that she is a comedienne of the highest quality and the attention in the Follies secures her star status. Nicky appears again and romance starts to blossom, although he keeps disappearing from her life due to various 'deals' he is involved with. Fanny decides to quit her show and run after Nicky. They marry, but soon Nicky starts to gamble too dangerously and loses his money, thereby leaving Fanny with no option but to pay

all the bills which make him look like he is living off her earnings. Nicky becomes involved in a fraudulent deal and is arrested. When he is released from prison he returns to Fanny to tell her that their life together is over.

Don't Rain On My Parade is sung when Fanny decides to walk out of the show in which she is appearing to follow Nicky and spend her life with him. The recording used in this book is based on the original 1964 Broadway cast album as sung by Barbra Streisand (*EMI Records – ZDM 7 64661 2 5*).

Funny Girl opened on Broadway in 1964 and ran for 1,348 performances. The London production only ran for 112 performances as Miss Streisand had to leave the show when she became pregnant. The film was made in 1968. Due to the fact that the show is so allied to the memorable performance of Barbra Streisand, the show has never had a major revival.

A Star Is Born (1976)
Screenplay by John Gregory Dunne, Joan Didion and Frank Pierson

John Norman Howard, a rock star whose star celebratory is falling fast, has become jaded with the music business and is going down the slippery slope of drink and drugs. One evening he spots singer Esther Hoffman performing in a local nightclub and is immediately taken with her and her talent. He approaches her and asks if he can help her career by showing her how to become a star. She agrees and together they work on songs and eventually fall in love with one another. Their happiness is spoiled by John's personal difficulties - his carelessness when dealing with journalists, failure to keep agreements with his agent and his occasional violence. Much to the aggravation of his manager, John makes Esther sing to his audience at one of his gigs. She is a success and gains a recording contract. It is the breakthrough she needed and as John's career dwindles, Esther's sky-rockets. She becomes a star and although she tries her utmost to stop John's decline, she cannot stop his self-destruction. One morning he drives away (whilst drinking beer) and becomes involved in an accident which kills him.

Evergreen is the love song from *A Star Is Born* and was co-written by Miss Streisand with a lyric by Paul Williams. The recording used in this book is based on the Columbia Records album (*506360 2*) The song won two Grammys and an Academy Award.

A Star Is Born was released in 1976 and was a box-office success.

Lynn Kellogg
Easy To Be Hard from *Hair*

Lynn Kellogg (b 1944) – Miss Kellogg can hardly be called a 'Legendary Lady of Broadway' because she only appeared in one show – but that show happened to be the groundbreaking musical *Hair* and she introduced one of its many enduring hit songs. Miss Kellogg made her Broadway debut in *Hair* (1968) paying the role of Sheila. When she left the show, her replacements included future Broadway names; Diane Keaton, Heather MacRae and Melba Moore. Prior to *Hair* Miss Kellogg was seen on various television entertainment shows and featured as the saloon girl Marcie in the Elvis Presley film *Charro!* (1969). More TV entertainment shows continued throughout the 1970s, sometimes appearing under the name of Lynn Ketchum. In later life, Miss Kellogg concentrated on singing Christian music.

Hair (1968)
Music by Galt MacDermot / Book and Lyrics by Gerome Ragni and James Rado

Hair, a virtually plotless musical, describes itself as "An American Tribal Love-Rock Musical". Berger, Claude and Sheila and a collection of long-haired young people are all members of 'The Tribe'. 'The Tribe' want to be free - they want to be able to do anything and think anything. Most particularly, they are totally against the Vietnam War and conscription. 'The Tribe' receive their conscription cards and decide to burn them along with the American flag. They also decide to take off all their clothes. Claude is the only member not to burn his draft card - he is not sure if he wants to go and so smokes marijuana to blot out thoughts of a decision. Claude wants Sheila, but Sheila wants Berger. Berger tells Sheila that he wants her to have sex with Claude as a farewell gift and as a gift to her he will have sex with her. The night before Claude leaves, Sheila decides to sleep with him. The next day, Claude, with his head shaved, leaves for the Army.

Easy To Be Hard is sung by Sheila after Berger has suggested that she has sex with Claude. The recording used in this book is based on the original 1968 Broadway cast album as sung by Lynn Kellogg (*Victor – 82876-56085-2*).

Hair originally opened in 1967 Off-Broadway. It was then altered and opened at Cheetah nightclub, before having further revisions and finally opening on Broadway in 1968 where it ran for 1,472 performances. *Hair* was a big phenomenon, because of its subject matter, its contemporary themes and because the cast appeared naked on the stage – the first time a whole cast had done so. The show transferred to London after the abolition of the Lord Chamberlain (who would have forbidden many things within the show) and it ran for 1,998 performances. A film was made in 1979.

Julia Migenes
Far From The Home I Love from *Fiddler On The Roof*

Julia Migenes (b 1949) – Singing star who has found success balancing a career between musical theatre, opera and the concert platform. Miss Migenes first played Broadway when she took over in the leading role of Lili in *Carnival!* (1963) and followed this by playing Maria in a 1964 revival of *West Side Story* at City Centre, New York. She created the role of Hodel in *Fiddler On The Roof* in 1964. Miss Migenes decided that singing was her calling and from thereon performed in opera and concerts. She played the title role in the 1984 film of *Carmen* (under the name of Julia Migenes-Johnson opposite Placido Domingo) and also the role of Jenny Diver in the 1990 film of *The Threepenny Opera* titled *Mack the Knife*. Miss Migenes has recorded many albums; musical theatre related including: **Man of La Mancha**, **Kismet** and **Rags**.

Fiddler on the Roof (1964)
Music by Jerry Bock / Lyrics by Sheldon Harnick / Book by Joseph Stein

Set in the Jewish village of Anatevka in czarist Russia of 1905, *Fiddler On The Roof* tells the story of Tevye, his wife and daughters. In a community steeped in tradition, it is normal for daughters to be married to husbands chosen by the village matchmaker. Tevye's eldest daughter, Tzeital, is set to marry a middle-aged butcher but she has already declared her love to her childhood sweetheart, the penniless tailor, Motel. After much anguish, she tells her father of this and he has to concoct a story (using the devise of a nightmare) to persuade his wife and the butcher that she cannot marry him. His other daughters also decide to marry men they love, rather than those chosen for them; his second daughter, Hodel, marries a revolutionary who is sent to Siberia and his third daughter, Chava, marries outside of her faith and is made an outcast from the family. The story is set against the background of impending danger as Jews are being driven out of Russia. As the musical ends, Tevye and the remainder of his family emigrate to America, to find a better life, but still holding on to their precious traditions.

Far From The Home I Love is sung by Hodel to her father Tevye as she decides to leave her family and her home to join her husband in Siberia. The recording used in this book is based on the original 1964 Broadway cast album as sung by Julia Migenes (*RCA Red Seal – RCD1-7060*).

Fiddler On The Roof opened in 1964 and was so successful that it became the longest ever running musical on Broadway at 3,242 performances. The London production was also triumphant, running for 2,030 performances. The show was made into a popular film in 1971, has been produced worldwide and constantly revived.

Lucille Ball
Hey, Look Me Over! from *Wildcat*

Lucille Ball (1911 - 1989) – Flaming red-headed comedienne, Lucille Ball was famous for her TV comedy show *I Love Lucy*, and was hugely popular with the American public. Lucille Ball only appeared in one Broadway musical – *Wildcat* (1960), but had made many musical films throughout the 40s (where her singing voice was usually dubbed) including: *Too Many Girls* (1941), *Du Barry was a Lady* (1943), *Best Foot Forward* (1943) and *Ziegfeld Follies* (1946). Throughout the 1950s, Miss Ball was almost a permanent fixture on television with her own show *I Love Lucy*. She returned to musical films in 1974 when she played the title role in *Mame*.

Wildcat (1960)
Music by Cy Coleman / Lyrics by Carolyn Leigh / Book by N. Richard Nash

Wildcat Jackson and her sister Janie are broke. They arrive in a town near the Mexican border which has discovered oil. Wildcat uses her natural charm and nerve to persuade the best drill foreman to work for her. His name is Joe and she also falls for him. She then tries to buy some land, and once she has managed to persuade a crew to work for her, begins to work on the property for oil. Joe believes that the oil-well is dry and decides to leave, so Wildcat tells the local Sheriff that Joe was involved in a brawl and killed a man. At his trial she acts as his defence and persuades the Sheriff to let Joe be put in her custody – then he would have no option but to work for her! Joe finds out that the man he hit in the brawl was not killed and walks out on Wildcat. Furious, she throws all his belongings into the well hole. Inadvertently, she has also thrown his dynamite down the hole which was hidden in his belongings. When Joe returns he realises what Wildcat has done and in a desperate attempt to get her away from the impending danger tells her that he loves her - just as the well explodes and blows a gusher of oil!

Hey, Look Me Over! is sung when Wildcat tells her sister Janie that if you always look on the positive side in the face of adversity, everything will turn out well! The recording used in this book is based on the original 1960 Broadway cast album as sung by Lucille Ball (*Celebrate Broadway Volume One, Sing Happy! – RCA Victor 09026-61987-2*).

Wildcat (1960) has an exciting musical score and produced a standard in **Hey, Look Me Over!**, however the show failed to have a long run on Broadway and closed after 171 performances.

Madeline Kahn
Never from *On The Twentieth Century*

Madeline Kahn (1942 - 1999) – A comedienne, possessing a singing voice of amazing vocal range, who found much success throughout theatre and film. Miss Kahn was first noticed on Broadway in *Leonard Sillman's New Faces of 1968* before creating the role of Goldie in *Two By Two* and nearly stealing the show from Danny Kaye! Miss Kahn went to Hollywood where she continued to steal the limelight in various films: Eunice in the film *What's Up, Doc?* and many Mel Brooks films; Lili Von Shtupp (the singing saloon singer) in *Blazing Saddles* (1974), Elizabeth in *Young Frankenstein* and Victoria in *High Anxiety* (1978). Miss Kahn returned to Broadway for a short period, creating the role of Lily Garland in the musical *On The Twentieth Century* (1978). TV and film followed and then she returned to Broadway in the plays; *Born Yesterday* (1989) and gained her first Tony Award in the play *The Sisters Rosenweig* (1993). Miss Kahn played the role of Cora in a concert version of the musical *Anyone Can Whistle* at Carnegie Hall in 1995.

On The Twentieth Century (1978)
Music by Cy Coleman / Book and Lyrics by Betty Comden and Adolph Green

Oscar, a failing theatre producer and director, has just had another flop. He flees the theatre (without paying anyone) and boards the 'Twentieth Century', a luxury train bound for New York. He knows that film star Lily Garland is also boarding the train. Years before, he discovered Lily, transformed her into a star and became her lover before she left him and became a film star. He is hoping that he will be able to persuade her back to the theatre which will put him back on top! Stickers are being stuck all over the train saying 'Repent' which gives Oscar the idea of starring Lily in a play about Mary Magdalene. Lily will have nothing of it. The stickers are the work of Mrs. Primrose, a rich elderly lady, who Oscar persuades to back his play. When Lily hears that Oscar has found the backing for his show, she starts to warm towards the idea of playing Mary Magdalene — even more so when Oscar suggests that they also make it into a film – which Mrs. Primrose also agrees to back! At this point, everyone learns that Mrs. Primrose has escaped from an asylum and has written phoney checks! Lily is furious and decides to take an offer from another producer and Oscar decides to shoot himself! Mrs. Primrose grabs the gun from his hand but it goes off and although Oscar is unhurt, he uses the situation to ask Lily to honour his 'last request' and sign a contract to appear in his production about Mary Magdalene. She signs, he jumps up and proves he is still alive and she shows him that she has signed the contract 'Peter Rabbit'. They fall into each other's arms realising that they were meant for each other!

When Oscar asks Lily to be in his play, Lily responds by singing **Never**. The recording used in this book is based on the original 1978 Broadway cast album as sung by Madeline Kahn (*Sony Broadway – SK 35330*).

On The Twentieth Century opened on Broadway in 1978 and ran for 460 performances. It opened in London in 1980, starring Julia McKenzie, but only ran for 165 performances.

Angela Lansbury
Not While I'm Around from *Sweeney Todd*

Angela Lansbury (b 1925) – A singing actress with a career that has successfully bridged film, theatre and television to great acclaim. At the beginning of her career, Miss Lansbury found great success in many straight films including: *Gaslight* (1944), *The Picture of Dorian Gray* (1945) and also a few musical films: *The Harvey Girls* (1946) and *Till The Clouds Roll By* (1946). More films continued throughout the 1950s before Miss Lansbury turned to Broadway in the plays *Hotel Paradiso* (1957) and the leading role of Helen in *A Taste of Honey* (1960). Miss Lansbury won acclaim in the film *The Manchurian Candidate* (1962) before reaching Broadway with her first musical role as Cora in the unsuccessful *Anyone Can Whistle* (1964). This was followed by the title role in *Mame* (1966 and revived in 1983) for which she won her first Tony Award. Her next Tony Award was won for the creation of Countess Aurelia in the musical *Dear World* (1969). Next was the musical film, *Bedknobs and Broomsticks* (1971), after which came Rose in *Gypsy* in London (1973), which she took to Broadway in 1974 and won another Tony. Her fourth Tony was won for creating the role of Mrs. Lovett in *Sweeney Todd* (1979 and TV broadcast 1982). Miss Lansbury played Ruth in the film of *The Pirates of Penzance* (1983) and then created her most famous role as Jessica Fletcher in the long running TV series *Murder, She Wrote* which commenced in 1983 until 1996 with occasional 'specials' in later years. Other musical roles continued on film as the voice of Mrs. Potts in Disney's *Beauty and the Beast* (1991) and the title role in the TV film *Mrs. Santa Claus* (1996). Miss Lansbury still appears in films and TV as well as hosting benefits, including a concert of *Anyone Can Whistle* in 1995.

Sweeney Todd (1979)
Music and Lyrics by Stephen Sondheim / Book by Hugh Wheeler

Sweeney Todd returns to London having been wrongly sentenced to 15 years in exile by a Judge who lusted after his wife and kept his child, Joanna. Sweeney sets up a barber shop above a pie shop run by Mrs. Lovett. Sweeney's friend, Anthony, finds Joanna and falls in love with her. He tries to save her, but his plan is heard by the Judge (who wants to keep Joanna and marry her himself) and so he hides her in an asylum. Frustrated that he nearly had his daughter back and nearly got his revenge on the Judge, Sweeney begins a killing spree. His victims are minced into pies by Mrs. Lovett, who has fallen for Sweeney. Eventually, Anthony finds Joanna and a plan is hatched: He rescues Joanna, tells the Judge she will be in Fleet Street, the Judge goes to Sweeney's shop and Sweeney gets his revenge with his barber's blade. Seemingly all is well, until it is revealed that Mrs. Lovett lied to Sweeney about his wife and he discovers that she was one of his victims. In a rage Sweeney throws Mrs. Lovett into her own oven and he is then killed by her shop-boy Tobias. Among the carnage, only Anthony and Joanna are left.

Mrs. Lovett sings to her simple shop-boy, Tobias, when he is frightened: **(No One's Going to Harm You) Not While I'm Around**.   The recording used in this book is based on the original 1979 Broadway cast album as sung by Angela Lansbury (*RCA Records – RCD1-5033*).

Sweeney Todd opened on Broadway in 1979 and ran for 557 performances. The London production ran for a disappointing 158 performances. The show has been revived many times in different forms, by opera companies, in concert productions and in small scale presentations.

....

Bernadette Peters
Raining In My Heart from *Dames At Sea*

Bernadette Peters (b 1948) - Known initially for her kewpie-doll looks and voice, has proved that she can handle roles of great maturity and is recognised as a great Broadway star. Bernadette Peters was first seen in a featured role on Broadway in *George M!* (1968) before she was catapulted to stardom as Ruby in the Off-Broadway musical spoof *Dames At Sea* (1968). Her next musical was a one-performance Broadway disaster, *La Strada* (1969), but she followed this with the role of Hildy in a revival of *On The Town* (1971) and then created the role of Mabel in *Mack and Mabel* (1974). A brief spell in Hollywood musicals followed with Eileen in *Pennies From Heaven* (1981) and Lily in *Annie* (1982). Broadway again beckoned: Dot in *Sunday in the Park with George* (1984 and TV 1986), Emma in *Song and Dance* (1985 - when Miss Peters won her first Tony Award), the Witch in *Into the Woods* (1987 and TV 1991), Paula in *The Goodbye Girl* (1993), the title role in the 1999 revival of *Annie Get Your Gun* (for which she won her second Tony) and lastly the mammoth role of Rose in the 2003 revival of *Gypsy*.

Dames At Sea (1968)
Music by Jim Wise / Book and Lyrics by Robin Miller and George Haimsohn

Broadway in the 1930s. Hennessey, a producer of Broadway musicals has had a run of 12 flops – but he's hoping his new show, *Dames At Sea*, will be a hit. In the middle of rehearsals a young lady walks into the theatre. She is called Ruby, has just stepped off the bus from her hometown of Centreville and wants to be in a Broadway show! Fortunately for her, a dancer has just eloped with a millionaire playboy, so Ruby gets into the chorus! Dick, a sailor on shore leave, arrives at the theatre too. He writes songs, much to the interest of the star of the show, Mona, who admires his talent - and his looks! Ruby and Dick bump into each other and instantly fall in love. Everything looks peachy, until Hennessey hears the news that his theatre has been sold! The future looks bleak. As the theatre is being bulldozed, Dick has the idea of staging the show on board his battleship – the Captain of which is an old flame of Mona's! Rehearsals go well on the ship, although Mona is making eyes at Dick, much to the distress of Ruby. A plot is hatched; Mona is made to feel sea sick and leaves the ship! A new star is needed and Ruby steps from the chorus line into the leading role! Thirteen must be Hennessey's lucky number as the show is a hit, Ruby becomes a Broadway star and everyone gets married!

Raining In My Heart is sung by Ruby after she has seen Mona in a clinch with Dick and she is upset! The recording used in this book is based on the original 1969 Off-Broadway cast album as sung by Bernadette Peters (*Sony Broadway – SK 48214*).

Dames at Sea was conceived as a short one-act musical spoofing the Hollywood Musicals of the 1930s (*42nd Street*, *Golddiggers*, etc). It was enlarged to a two-act musical and opened Off-Broadway in 1969, running for 575 performances. The 1969 London production, featuring Sheila White as Ruby, was less successful, running for 127 performances. A TV production, made in 1971 featured Ann-Margret as Ruby. The show is constantly revived and performed throughout the world.

....

Gwen Verdon
Roxie from *Sweet Charity*

Gwen Verdon (1926 - 2000) – A vivacious dancer, singer and actress who had the ability to be both sexy and vulnerable in her many stage roles. After assisting choreographer Jack Cole in Hollywood and Broadway, Miss Verdon appeared as a dancer in a few lesser known musicals and films, before she was given the small role of Claudine in Cole Porter's *Can-Can* (1953) in which she nightly stole the show and won a Tony Award. She was then offered the role of Lola in *Damn Yankees* (1955) where she once again walked away with the show, won another Tony Award and re-created the role in the film version in 1958. *Damn Yankees* was choreographed by Bob Fosse who was becoming regarded as the most important choreographer of his generation. They married and he choreographed her in every other show in which she performed. Other musicals followed: *New Girl In Town* (1957) and *Redhead* (1959) for both of which she won Tony Awards. Her biggest success was in the title role of *Sweet Charity* (1966) in which she introduced *If My Friends Could See Me Now*. Her last musical role was Roxie in *Chicago* (1975). Although she did not perform in any more stage musicals, Miss Verdon appeared in many films in later life and supervised revivals of the work of Bob Fosse - most notably the Broadway production *Fosse* (1999).

Chicago (1975)
Music by John Kander / Lyrics by Fred Ebb / Book by Fred Ebb and Bob Fosse

For details of *Chicago*, see **And All That Jazz** (Chita Rivera). The recording used in this book is based on the Miramax Motion Picture album (*Epic – 510532 2*).

Mary Martin
Something Has Happened from *I Do! I Do!*

Mary Martin (1913 - 1990) – An ever youthful, lively, bubbly soubrette who became one of Broadway's most loved performers. Mary Martin became an overnight star in her Broadway debut, introducing Cole Porter's **My Heart Belongs To Daddy** in *Leave It To Me* (1938). A couple of flop musicals and some modest film performances immediately followed, until Miss Martin found great success back on Broadway in *One Touch of Venus* (1943), and *Lute Song* (1946). A brief stay in London for Noel Coward's *Pacific 1860* (1947) was an unhappy experience and she returned to America touring in *Annie Get Your Gun* which prompted Rodgers and Hammerstein to cast her in one of the biggest triumphs of her career as Nellie Forbush in *South Pacific* (1949) for which she won a Tony Award and then recreated the role in London in (1951). The role she will be ever remembered for is her Tony Award winning *Peter Pan* (1954) which she recreated live on TV in black and white in 1955 and 1956 and taped for posterity in colour in 1960. Mary Martin saw a German film of the life story of Maria von Trapp and immediately saw its potential as a musical and encouraged Rodgers and Hammerstein to join her. The result is one of the world's most loved musicals: *The Sound of Music* (1959) for which she won another Tony Award. Following this huge success, Miss Martin found herself in a musical that had a gorgeous score, but was a flop: *Jennie* (1963). She followed this by playing the title role in *Hello, Dolly* in London (1965) and then created her final role on Broadway as Agnes in the successful two-handed musical: *I Do! I Do!* (1966). Miss Martin continued her career with occasional TV and stage appearances. She is also well-known as the mother of Larry Hagman - JR in *Dallas*!

I Do! I Do! (1966)
Music by Harvey Schmidt / Book and Lyrics by Tom Jones

Staged entirely on one set - a symbolic four poster bed - *I Do! I Do!* charts the married life of Michael and Agnes. Opening with their youthful wedding, the show continues through early married life, the birth of two children, Michael's success in business – and his affair, Agnes's home life difficulties and forgiveness of his affair, worrying about their teenage children, the closeness of being alone together after their children's marriages and ultimately leaving their family home – and their four poster bed.

Something Has Happened is sung when Agnes realises she is pregnant. The recording used in this book is based on the original 1966 Broadway cast album as sung by Mary Martin (*RCA Victor – 1128-2-RC*).

I Do! I Do! is a musical that only features two performers. The original Broadway cast were both stars – Mary Martin and Robert Preston and were succeeded by Carol Lawrence and Gordon MacRae. The show opened in 1966 and ran for 561 performances. The London production starring Anne Rogers and Ian Carmichael ran for 115 performances in 1968 followed by a revival in 1976 with Juliet Prowse and Rock Hudson. An American touring production starring Lee Remick and Hal Linden was televised in 1982.

....

Rita Gardner
Soon It's Gonna Rain from *The Fantasticks*

Rita Gardner – mainly known for her portrayal as Luisa in *The Fantasticks*, had a successful career on Broadway, Off-Broadway, in regional theatre and in cabaret. Following *The Fantasticks*, Miss Gardener played Broadway, creating the role of Sally in the unsuccessful musical *A Family Affair* in 1962. Her Broadway career then continued replacing or understudying various leading roles in musicals and plays – most notably: *Ben Franklyn In Paris* (1964/5), *On A Clear Day You Can See Forever* (1965), *Last of the Red Hot Lovers* (1969) and the flop musical *Ari* (1971). Miss Gardner played Off-Broadway in *Jacques Brel is Alive and Well and Living In Paris* and *To Be Young Gifted and Black* and in later life created her own one-woman show celebrating the Off-Broadway musical. Miss Gardner has played various roles in straight plays in regional theatres, including a new musical: *Eleanor: A Love Story* (Washington: 1999).

The Fantasticks (1960)
Music by Harvey Schmidt / Book and Lyrics by Tom Jones

Luisa and Matt live next to each other. They are in love, but their fathers do not like each other and have built a wall between the two gardens. In actual fact, the fathers do like each other, but they think that if they have a wall and forbid their siblings to see each other it will encourage them to do the opposite and become partners! They employ a travelling showman to stage an abduction of Luisa and he will then let Matt catch him and rescue Luisa. The plan works well; Luisa and Matt openly declare their love and the fathers pull down the wall. All goes well until the lovers realise they have been tricked. The rot sets in; the wall is re-built, Luisa falls for the charms of the showman and Matt leaves the village and discovers a world of misery and hurt. Luisa is dumped, Matt returns and both realise that they are now ready for a mature relationship. All ends happily and although the fathers decide to take down the wall again, everyone decides that it is best if it remains!

Soon It's Gonna Rain is a duet between Matt and Luisa and appears in the show when the lovers meet before an impending storm - and just before Luisa is abducted. The recording used in this book is based on the original 1960 Off-Broadway cast album as sung by Rita Gardner and Kenneth Nelson (*Decca Broadway – 314 543 665-2*).

Following its opening in 1960 at the Off-Broadway Sullivan Street Playhouse, *The Fantasticks* became the longest running musical in the world, closing in 2001 after 16,875 performances. A TV production was aired in 1964 and a film was eventually made in 1996/7 and released in 2000 but was unsuccessful. The London production only ran for 44 performances in 1961.

AND ALL THAT JAZZ
(from *Chicago*)

Words by John Kander
Music by Fred Ebb

Backing

DON'T RAIN ON MY PARADE
(from *Funny Girl*)

Words by Bob Merrill
Music by Jule Styne

Brightly

Don't tell___ me not to live, just sit and put-ter life's can-dy and the sun's a ball of but-ter don't bring___ a-round a cloud to rain on my par - ade___

HEY, LOOK ME OVER
(from *Wildcat*)

Words by Carolyn Leigh
Music by Cy Coleman

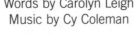

Backing

EASY TO BE HARD
(from *Hair*)

Words by James Rado and Gerome Ragni
Music by Galt MacDermot

Backing

EVERGREEN
(from *A Star Is Born*)

Words and Music by Barbra Streisand and Paul Williams

FAR FROM THE HOME I LOVE
(from *Fiddler On The Roof*)

Words by Sheldon Harnick
Music by Jerry Bock

Slowly, pensively

How can I hope to make you un-der-stand why I do what I do,

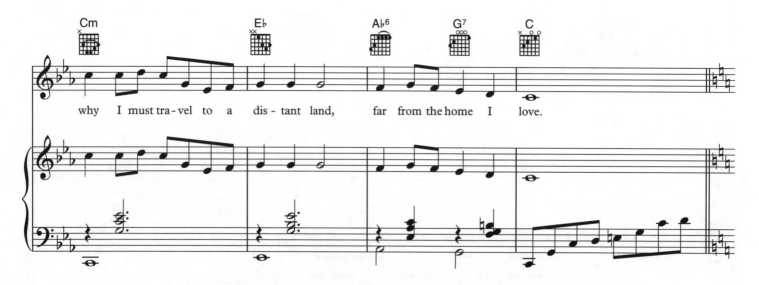

why I must tra-vel to a dis-tant land, far from the home I love.

NEVER
(from *On The 20th Century*)

Words by Betty Comden and Adolph Green
Music by Cy Coleman

Let me see, let me see, he wants me to come back to him.

When could that date be? March, Sep-tem-ber, June, No-vem-ber, you tell him from me.

40

NOT WHILE I'M AROUND
(from *Sweeney Todd*)

Words and Music by Stephen Sondheim

Backing

No - thing's gon - na harm you,

not while I'm a - round. No - thing's gon - na harm you, no sir,

not while I'm a - round. De - mons are prowl - ing ev - 'ry - where,

Backing

RAINING IN MY HEART
(from *Dames At Sea*)

Words by George Haimsohn and Robin Miller
Music by Jim Wise

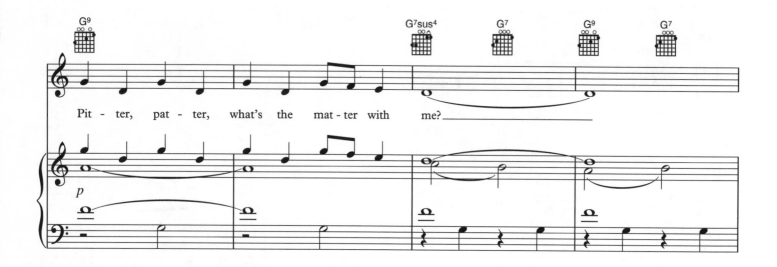

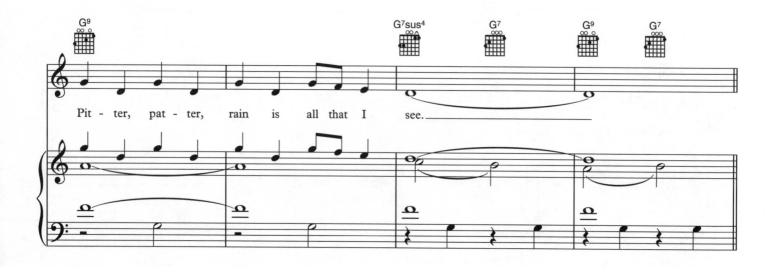

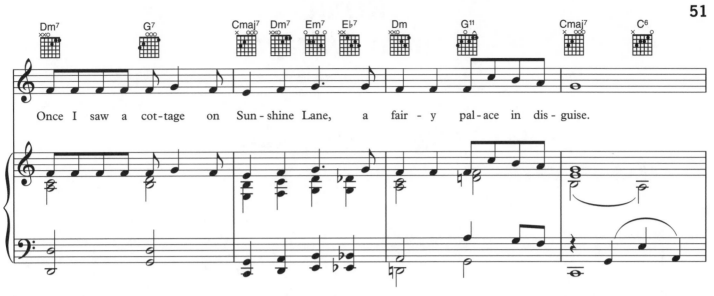

Once I saw a cot-tage on Sun-shine Lane, a fair-y pal-ace in dis-guise.

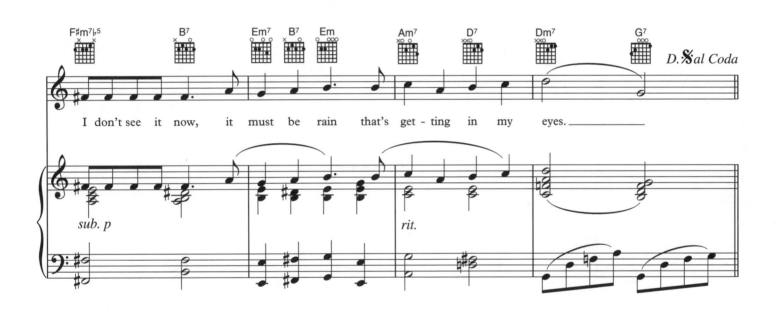

I don't see it now, it must be rain that's get-ting in my eyes. _____

sub. p　　　　　　　　*rit.*

D. %al Coda

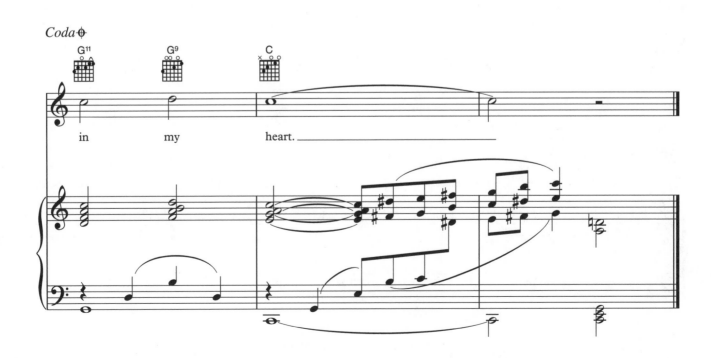

Coda

in my heart. _____

Backing

ROXIE
(from *Chicago*)

Words by Fred Ebb
Music by John Kander

SOMETHING HAS HAPPENED
(from *I Do, I Do*)

Words by Tom Jones
Music by Harvey Schmidt

Backing

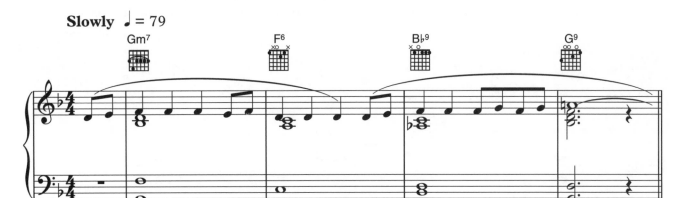

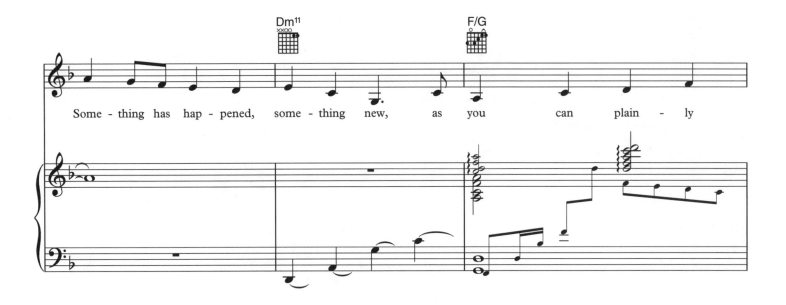

Some-thing has hap-pened, some-thing new, as you can plain-ly

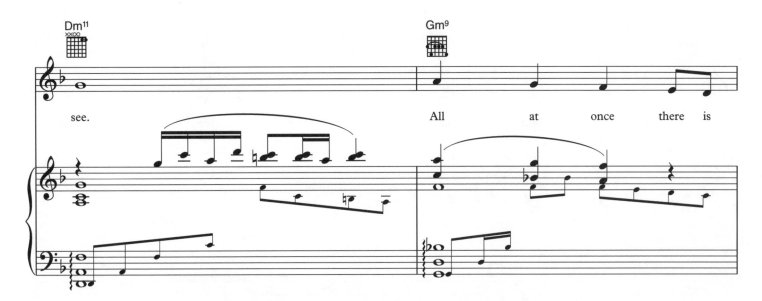

see. All at once there is

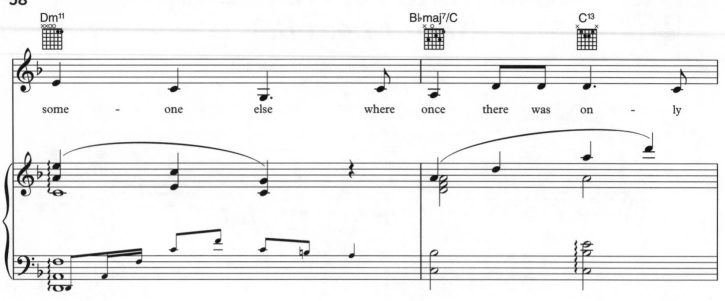

some - one else where once there was on - ly

Più mosso

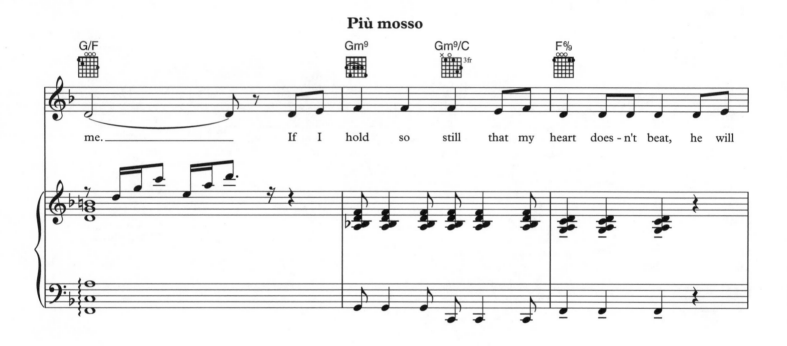

me. _____ If I hold so still that my heart does - n't beat, he will

some - times kick me gent - ly with his feet. Oh,

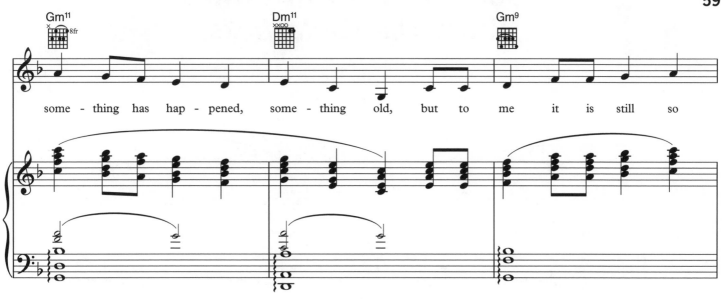

some-thing has hap-pened, some-thing old, but to me it is still so

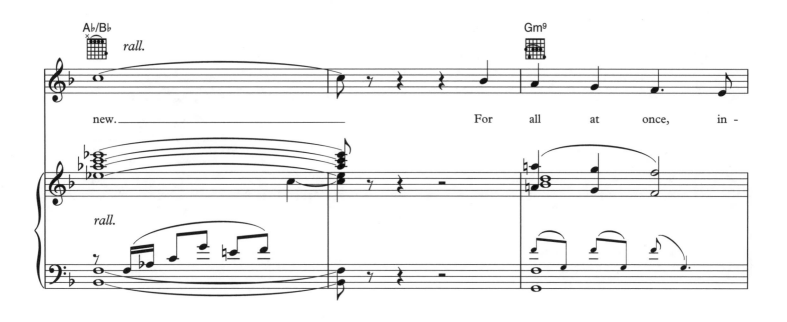

new._____ For all at once, in-

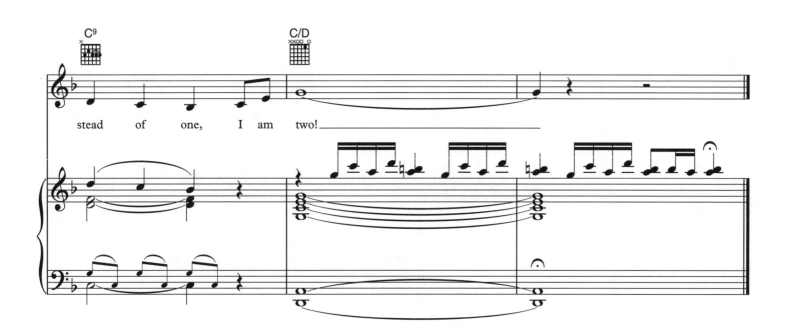

stead of one, I am two!_____

Backing

SOON IT'S GONNA RAIN
(from *The Fantasticks*)

Words by Tom Jones
Music by Harvey Schmidt

Moderato

Gently

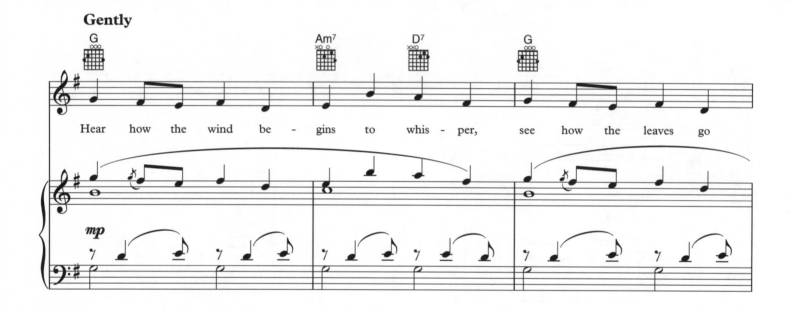

Hear how the wind be - gins to whis - per, see how the leaves go

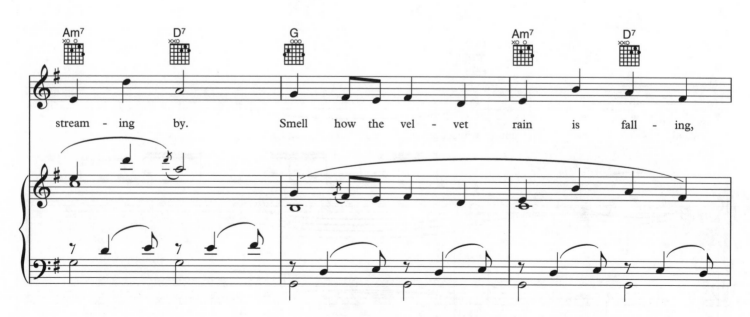

stream - ing by. Smell how the vel - vet rain is fall - ing,

62

Refrain

stay.

Soon it's gon - na rain; I can see it. Soon it's gon - na rain;

I can tell. Soon it's gon - na rain,

what are we gon - na do?